Forewc

We're so lucky in the UK becaus treasures just waiting to be discove..... .... Devon's 'Jurassic Coast' to Norfolk's 'Deep History Coast', our beaches are a great place to start looking for fossils. Fossil hunting is a fun, exciting and free hobby. It helps us to learn about the history of life on Earth and is a great way to begin to study the natural world. It also keeps us fit and healthy by being outdoors. There's nothing better than finding something that no one has ever seen before. Imagine being the first ever person to hold a fossil shell or sea-sponge that's hundreds of millions of years old - now that's really impressive!

Finding fossils is a mixture of skill and practice, with a bit of luck. A little secret is that young people are brilliant at finding fossils as you're closer to the ground than most grown-ups and you normally have much better eyesight! I wish this book was available when I was a child - I would have begged my parents to buy it for me! It will help you to identify and understand the most common fossils in the country. **Prehistoric minibeasts** are everywhere and the brilliant drawings and excellent information in this book will help you to be an expert in no time! Remember to collect fossils responsibly - don't take too many and don't leave a mess behind you.

Happy fossil hunting!

Dr David Waterhouse
Palaeontologist (fossil hunter)
and Museum Curator

Extraordinary Extinct™
Prehistoric Minibeasts
A First Guide to Fossils

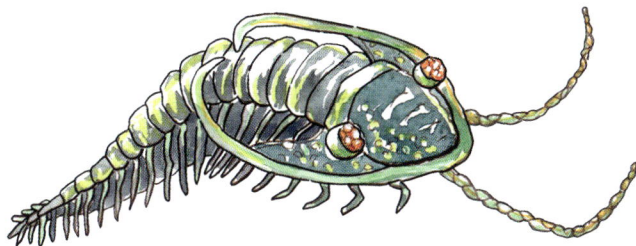

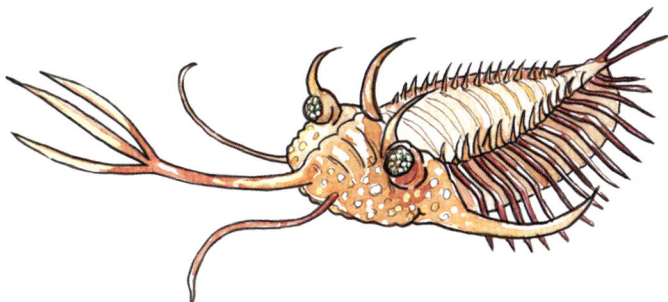

Jill Michelle Smith

and

Jennifer Watson

What is a minibeast?

A minibeast is a small **invertebrate** (an animal without a backbone or internal bone skeleton) such as a crab, butterfly, beetle, spider, slug, snail, squid or starfish.

This book focuses on **nine prehistoric minibeasts**. Alongside each type there is a specific example of an extraordinary extinct **fossil species** that is commonly found in the United Kingdom. With the help of this guide, young explorers can identify these distinctive fossils on beaches, in rocky areas, muddy fields and even gardens!

What is a fossil?

Fossils are the remains of ancient animals and plants that have been preserved by quickly being covered in sediment, such as mud or sand. Over a very long time, often millions of years, the animal or plant is replaced by minerals, which turns them into rock. These very particular conditions leave behind the **cast** of a living creature or their imprint in the rock, called a **mould**.

Cast

Mould

Here are some examples of minibeasts.
The fossil creatures in this book are <u>underlined</u>.

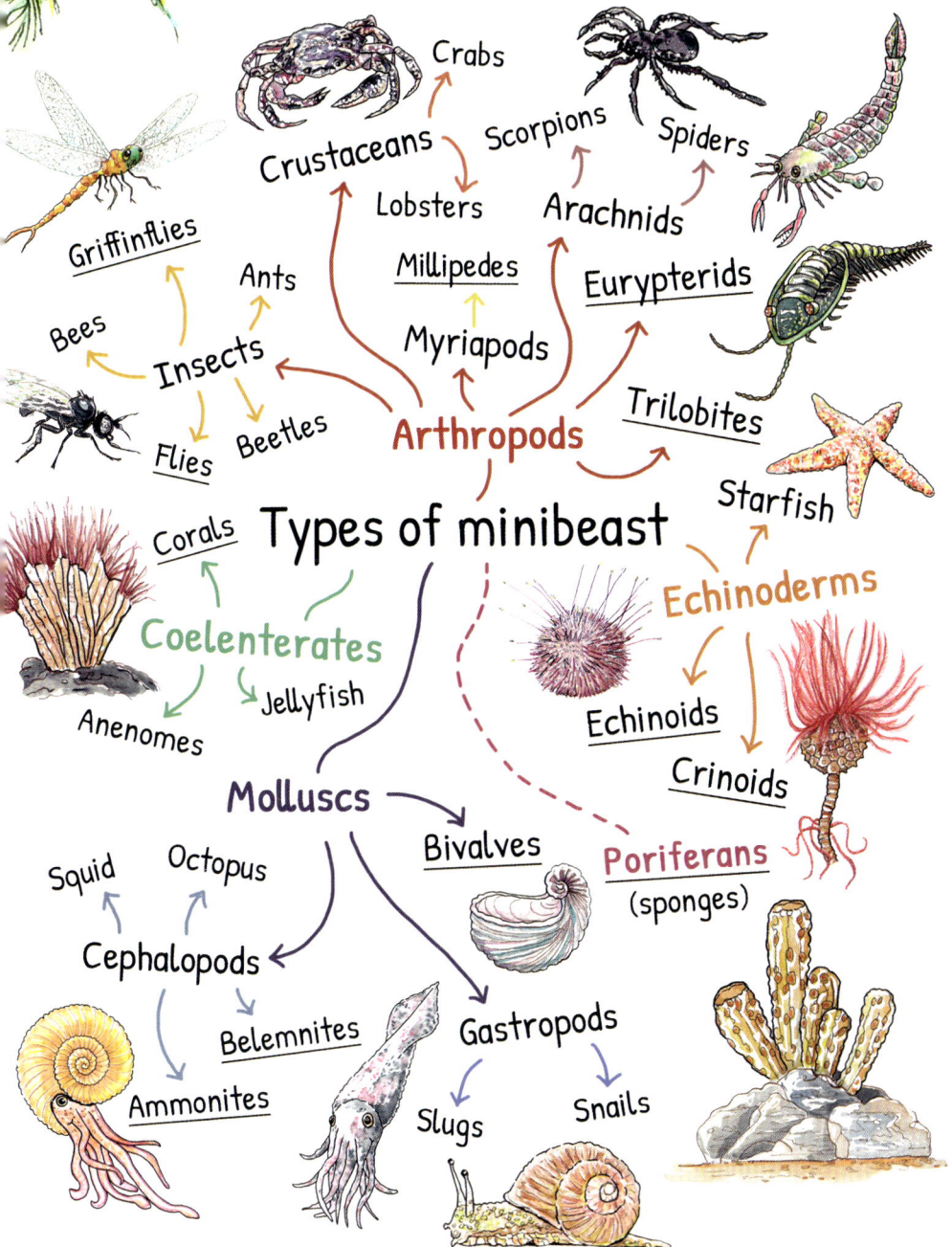

Types of minibeast

Arthropods

Crabs

Crustaceans

Lobsters

Scorpions

Spiders

Arachnids

<u>Eurypterids</u>

<u>Millipedes</u>

Myriapods

<u>Trilobites</u>

<u>Griffinflies</u>

Ants

Bees

Insects

Flies

Beetles

Starfish

Coelenterates

<u>Corals</u>

Anenomes

Jellyfish

Echinoderms

<u>Echinoids</u>

<u>Crinoids</u>

Molluscs

Squid

Octopus

Cephalopods

Bivalves

Poriferans
(sponges)

Belemnites

Gastropods

<u>Ammonites</u>

Slugs

Snails

Ammonites

Ammonites were a very varied group of squid-like sea creatures, which existed for over 150 million years. Their shell fossils have been found all over the world and were first named by a Roman philosopher, after the Egyptian god Ammon.

The Anglo Saxons called ammonites 'snakestones'.

What can you find?

Ammonites can be found on beaches across the UK and even in gardens or fields where the sea level once was!

Thousands of ammonite species have been discovered, ranging from just a centimetre in size to 2 metres in diameter!

Ammonite

Pronounced: *ah-moh-nite*
Lived: Jurassic to Cretaceous
Size: up to 6 metres long
Diet: Plankton, crustaceans and bivalves
First documented: Italy, 79 CE

Daisy the
Dactylioceras

Pronounced: *dak-tay-lee-oh-seh-rass*

Extinct: 180 million years ago   Size: 7 centimetres long

A marvellous marine mollusc of the Jurassic seas,
Daisy bobbed backwards through the water with ease!
She was quite a small species of ammonite,
But her coiling ribbed shell was strong and bright.
Her eight flexible tentacles propelled her on her way,
As she scavenged for food on the ocean floor each day.

Belemnites

Although belemnite finds have been recorded for over 2,000 years, they were first recognised as fossils in 1546. The name 'belemnite' comes from the Greek word for 'dart', because of the pointy shape of their fossils.

The part of these squid-like creatures that is often found fossilised is called a 'guard'. It comes from inside the pointy tip of the animal.

What can you find?

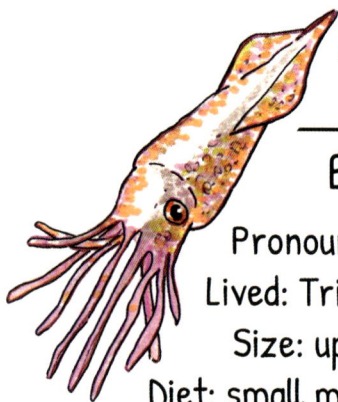

Look out for cylinder-shaped belemnite fossils on beaches, coastal paths and among gravel!

guard

Belemnite

Pronounced: *bell-am-nite*
Lived: Triassic to Cretaceous
Size: up to 5 metres long
Diet: small marine creatures and fish
First documented: Greece, 400 BCE

Benji the Belemnitella

Pronounced: *bell-am-nit-ella*

Extinct: 66 million years ago   Size: 18 centimetres long

Benji dipped and dived in the Late Cretaceous seas,
Using his ten long strong arms to swim at speed!
He was a streamlined squid-shaped cephalopod,
With his shell on the inside, which might seem odd.
But this structure makes fossils like his easy to find,
Looking like little stone bullets upon the shoreline.

Trilobites

Trilobites were ancient ancestors of modern minibeasts. They first appeared over half a billion years ago and went extinct long before dinosaurs evolved on Earth.

There were many types of trilobite. Some had antennae, some had spines and others could roll up like woodlice!

What can you find?

In the UK, trilobites are found in coastal and mountain rocks, particularly in the West Midlands and Wales.

Hundreds of years ago, some Native American tribes would wear trilobite fossils as amulets to protect against illness.

Trilobite

Pronounced: *try-loh-bite*
Lived: Cambrian to Permian
Size: up to 70 centimetres long
Diet: Small animals, such as worms
First documented: Wales, 1698

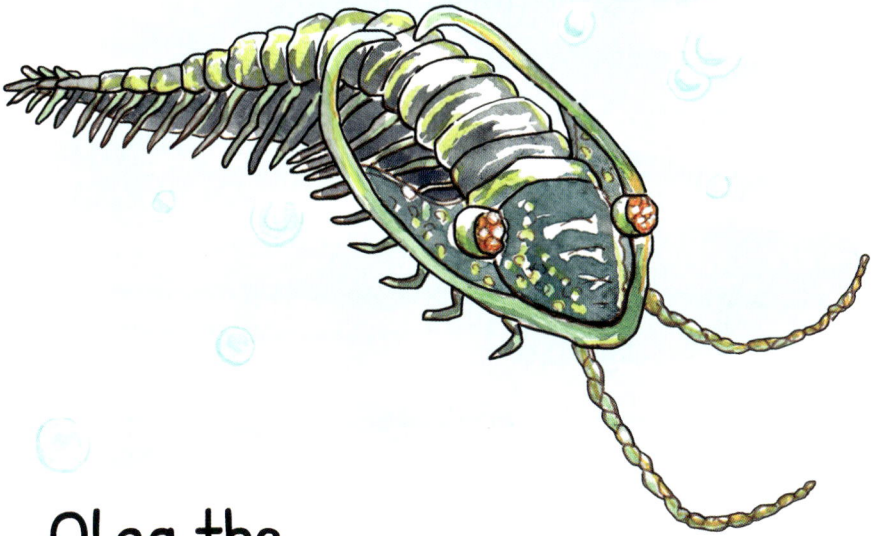

Olga the
Ogyginus

Pronounced: *og-ee-gee-nus*

Extinct: 252 million years ago   Size: 6 centimetres long

Olga was an ancient arthropod discovered in Wales,
She had a thorax, body and pygidium tail.
Like an alien creature, she would've been an unusual sight,
But was actually one of twenty thousand trilobite types.
She swam, scuttled and scavenged in the deep dark seas,
Her hard outer skeleton stopped her being a predator's tea!

Echinoids

Echinoids are a group of marine animals including sea urchins and sand dollars. They first evolved at the end of the Ordovician Period, 450 million years ago and by the Jurassic Period they came in many shapes and sizes.

Echinoids are some of the most beautiful fossils and their striking patterns make them easy to identify.

Echinoids are closely related to starfish and sea cucumbers!

What can you find?

Echinoid fossils are common on most British beaches, but are more easily found in places with chalk rock.

Echinoid

Pronounced: *ek-uh-noid*
Lived: Ordovician to present
Size: up to 40 centimetres with spines
Diet: algae and crustacean larvae
First documented: observed alive

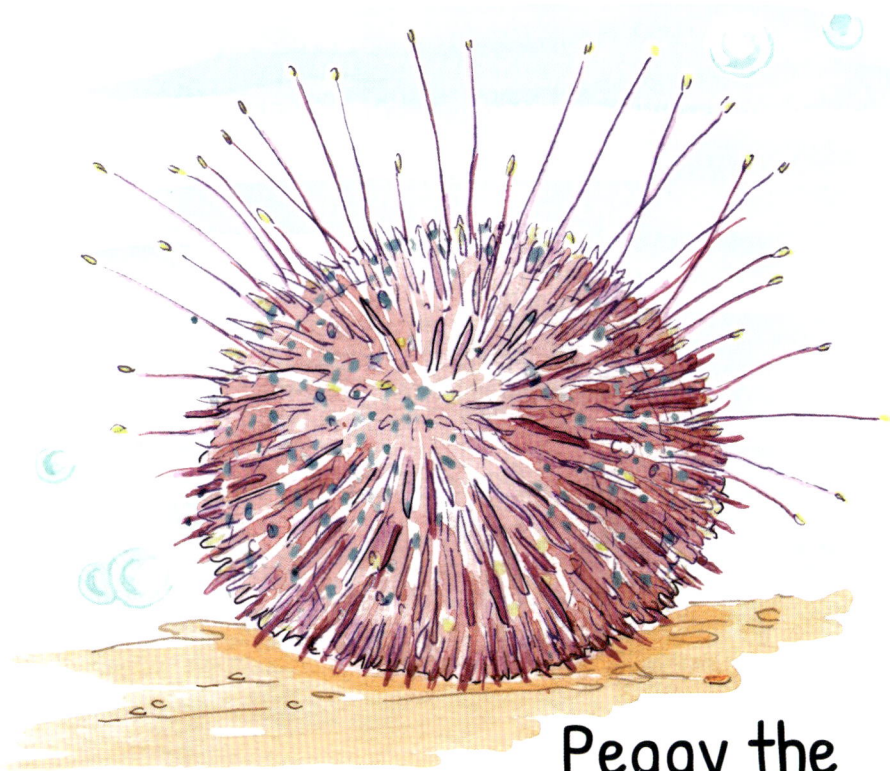

Peggy the

Pygurus

Pronounced: *pie-ger-as*

Extinct: 66 million years ago   Size: 12 centimetres wide

Peggy lived in shallow waters along an ancient coast,
Feasting on small particles, she enjoyed algae the most!
As her tube feet gripped tight to fight the ocean's swell,
She was kept safe by sharp spines on her spherical shell.
A Jurassic relative of today's sea urchins,
From chalk rock, fossils like hers are always emerging.

Crinoids

Crinoids are marine animals that first evolved in the Ordovician Period, 485 million years ago . Crinoids are stalked when they are young, which means they are attached to the sea floor. Some adult crinoids move to new locations by crawling, but others lose their stalk and float around freely.

Stalked crinoids are called 'sea lillies' and unstalked are called 'feather stars'.

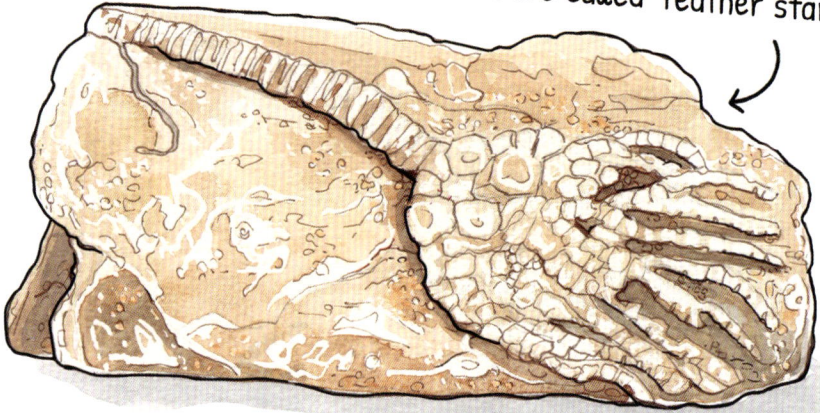

What can you find?

Star stones are tiny crinoid stalk fragments!

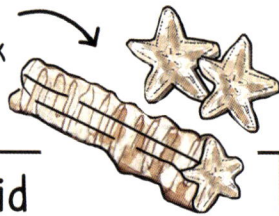

Star-shaped fragments of crinoids can be found on beaches across the UK. They are common in Yorkshire and Dorset.

Crinoid

Pronounced: *cry-noyd*
Lived: Ordovician to present
Size: up to 40 metres long
Diet: microorganisms such as plankton
First documented: observed alive

Dimitri the
Dimerocrinus

Pronounced: *dime-roh-cry-nus*

Extinct: 252 million years ago   Size: 6 centimetres tall

Dancing and swaying on the floor of the Permian sea,
Dimitri looked like a strange plant, a type of tiny tree.
In fact he was an animal in delicate flowery form,
With feathery arms to gather morsels from dusk until dawn!
Fine fossils like his are found in England to this very day,
A beautiful treasure hidden away in rocks, sand or clay.

Bivalves

Bivalves are common shellfish, such as clams and oysters. They are a very successful and ancient group of animals that have existed since the Cambrian Period, over 500 million years ago.

Bivalves were slow to evolve, but adapted so well that they haven't changed much over millions of years.

Their shells have two halves called 'valves'.

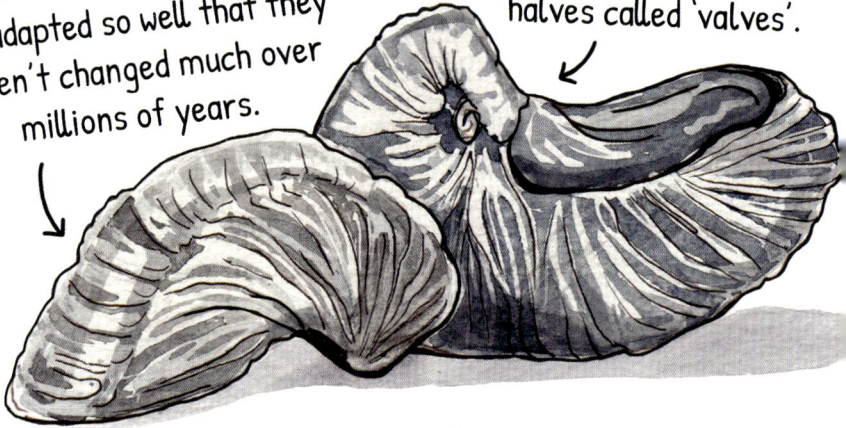

Fossil species like Gryphea, are often called 'devil's toenails' because of their claw-like shape!

What can you find?

In the UK, bivalve fossils are commonly found on beaches, as well as in muddy fields in the East Midlands.

Bivalve

Pronounced: *bai-valv*
Lived: Cambrian to present
Size: up to 1.4 metres long
Diet: particles of food in water
First documented: observed alive

Gary the

Gryphaea

Pronounced: *gry-fee-ah*

Extinct: 46 million years ago   Size: 7 centimetres long

A common oyster in the shallows of Triassic oceans,
Gary crowded with his colony, hardly showing any motion.
He had a gnarly-shaped shell in which he lived,
And another flat shell he used for a lid.
From Northeast England his fossils often hail,
Unflatteringly named a 'devil's toenail'!

Sponges

Thousands of sponge species have been discovered and the oldest sponge relative dates back to 850 million years ago, making them the most ancient known creatures on Earth. Believe it or not, all flint rocks are made from silica, which is a product of fossilised sponges.

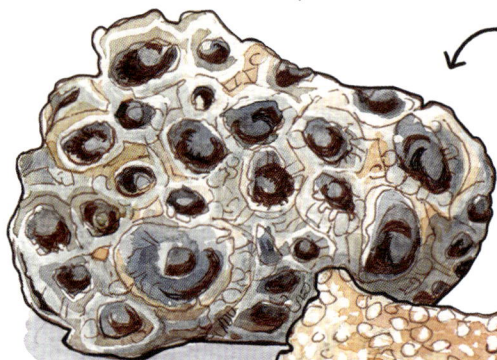

Sponges are also known as 'Poriferans' meaning 'to have pores', as they are covered in tiny holes!

Sponges come in all shapes and sizes. Most species live in the sea and many build reefs, which are home to other marine animals.

What can you find?

You can find fossil sponges in flint everywhere, from beaches and fields to stone walls and gravel drives.

Porifera

Pronounced: *por-if-er-ah*
Lived: Precambrian to present
Size: up to 3.5 metres tall
Diet: microorganisms such as plankton
First documented: observed alive

Vera the
Ventriculite

Pronounced: *ven-trik-yul-ite*

Extinct: 66 million years ago   Size: 12 centimetres tall

Vera might not seem much like a living creature,
Because she lacked typical bodily features.
Without a brain or a mouth, nose, ears or eyes,
She absorbed food from the sea to keep her alive.
Despite looking like a cactus under the waves and surf,
Sponges were surprisingly the first animals on Earth!

Corals

A coral is made up of a group of tiny individual animals called polyps, which are each only a few centimetres tall. The Silurian Period is sometimes called "the age of corals" because so many different species thrived at that time.

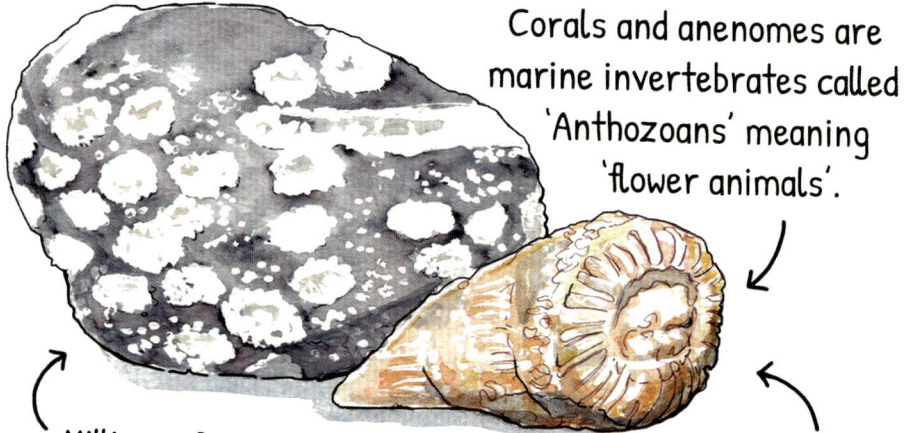

Corals and anenomes are marine invertebrates called 'Anthozoans' meaning 'flower animals'.

Millions of years ago, much more of the Earth's surface was covered with water and so huge coral reefs formed, such as the Wenlock fossil reef on the border of Wales!

Rugosa coral fossils are horn-shaped.

What can you find?

Coral fossils come in many shapes, but dark pebbles with white dots are often quite easy to spot on British beaches.

Anthozoa

Pronounced: *an-tho-zoa*
Lived: Cambrian to present
Size: up to 13 metres wide
Diet: plankton, algae and small fish
First documented: observed alive

Serina the

Syringopora

Pronounced: *suh-ring-oh-por-ah*

Extinct: 279 million years ago   Size: 2 centimetres tall

Serina was one of hundreds in her coral colony,
As part of a tenacious team, she had excellent company.
Her teeny tiny tentacles waited for the perfect dish,
Using her poisonous sting cells to stun plankton and fish.
Although her little polyp mouth opened readily for more,
She really was an incredibly inconspicuous carnivore!

Flies

'Diptera' is the name for the group of insects that includes flies, mosquitos and gnats. These arthropods first evolved in the Triassic Period and over time have been trapped and fossilised in sticky tree resin called amber.

Remarkably, 48-million-year-old amber from Scandanavia can be found on beaches in Norfolk and Suffolk!

What can you find?

Amber is often found among washed up seaweed and usually comes in translucent, dark orange pieces.

Older amber, containing insects that lived at the same time as the dinosaurs, has been found on the Isle of Wight.

Diptera

Pronounced: *dip-tuh-ruh*
Lived: Triassic to present
Size: up to 8 centimetres long
Diet: plant and animal juices
First documented: observed alive

Mika the
Microphorites

Pronounced: *mike-roh-foe-rai-teez*

Extinct: 33 million years ago   Size: 1.5 centimetres long

Mika and his family survived beyond dinosaur times,
And until the Eocene Epoch, they were common flies.
Wildly weaving through the forest looking for a snack,
He was ready to catch aphids who were drinking the sap.
Alas one day, in sticky tree resin, he ran out of luck,
Forever fossilised in amber, he would be stuck!

Giant Minibeasts

Unlike minibeasts found today, some prehistoric species were colossal. Here are some of the most impressive!

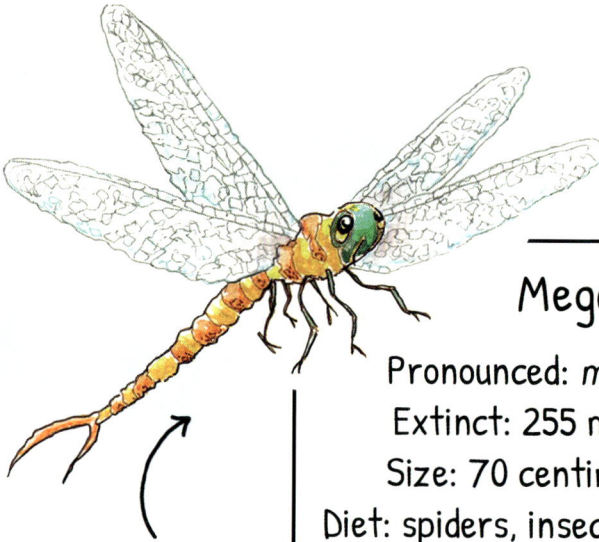

Meganeura was a type of griffinfly the size of a seagull!

Meganeura

Pronounced: *meg-ah-nyoo-rah*
Extinct: 255 million years ago
Size: 70 centimetres wingspan
Diet: spiders, insects and small animals
Discovered: France, 1880

Meganeura had huge eyes to help them find their prey!

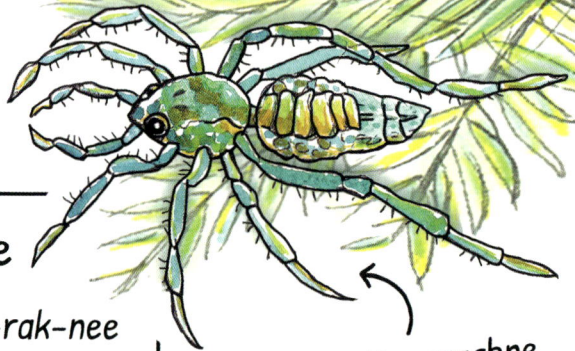

Megarachne

Pronounced: *meg-ah-rak-nee*
Extinct: 298 million years ago
Size: 50 centimetres long
Diet: small invertebrates
Discovered: Argentina, 1980

Although Megarachne looked like a spider, it was actually a type of sea scorpion!

More than 100 million years before the first dinosaurs evolved, the world was already brimming with enormous invertebrates! The largest were giant millipede-like arthropods and eurypterids, also known as sea scorpions.

Arthropleura

Pronounced: *ar-thro-ploo-rah*
Extinct: 290 million years ago
Size: 2.6 metres long
Diet: leaves, rotting foliage and wood
Discovered: Germany, 1854

Gigantic *Arthropleura* fossils have been found in Scotland and England!

The smallest eurypterids were a few centimetres long, but the largest reached over 2 metres!

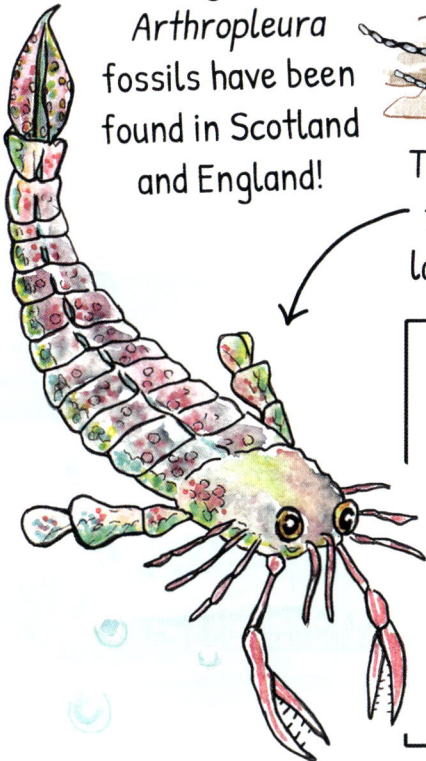

Jaekelopterus

Pronounced: *jay-kel-op-ter-us*
Extinct: 390 million years ago
Size: 2.5 metres long
Diet: fish, trilobites, ammonites and smaller eurypterids
Discovered: Germany, 1914

EXTRAORDINARY EXTINCT ™
Explorer Checklist

Here is a checklist of the prehistoric minibeast fossils in this book. You can use it to record your own finds!

Echinoid fossil ☐

What to look for: a rounded stone with patterns.

Where found: _____

When found: _____

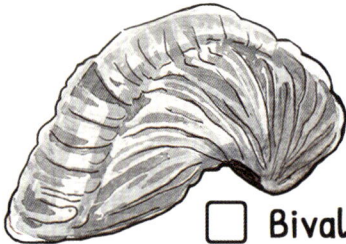

☐ Belemnite guard fossil

What to look for: smooth cylinder-shaped stones.

Where found: _____

When found: _____

☐ Bivalve fossil

What to look for: a shell-shaped stone with a ridged texture.

Where found: _____

When found: _____

Ammonite shell fossil ☐

What to look for: if not found loose among rocks and pebbles, a raised line running evenly around a smooth nodule sometimes indicates a fossil inside.

Where found: _____

When found: _____

☐ Coral fossil

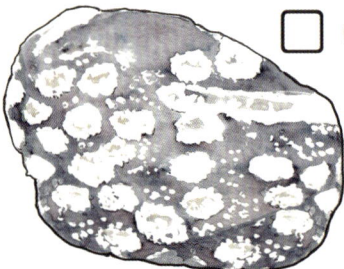

What to look for: a pebble with white dots. These dots are the tiny coral polyps.

Where found: _____

When found: _____

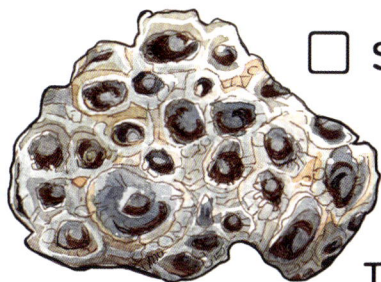

☐ **Sponge fossil**

What to look for: a flint with holes!

Where found: _____

When found: _____

Trilobite fossil ☐

What to look for: a bumpy shape, a bit like a large woodlouse.

Where found: _____

When found: _____

☐ **Crinoid stem fossils**

What to look for: tiny star-shaped fragments.

Where found: _____

When found: _____

Amber (fossilised tree resin) ☐

What to look for: Orange, translucent (almost see-through) smooth pieces among seaweed and recently washed up debris. It will feel light and float in salt water! If it doesn't, you might have found a gemstone, such as **carnelian** or **sard**.

Where found: _____

When found: _____

Discover the Extraordinary Extinct™ emporium...

dodoanddinosaur.com

EXTRAORDINARY EXTINCT™

Prehistoric Minibeasts
A First Guide to Fossils

First published in the UK in 2023

Text copyright © 2023 Jill Michelle Smith and Jennifer Watson
Illustrations copyright © 2023 Jill Michelle Smith
Copyright © 2023 Dodo and Dinosaur®

Written by Jill Michelle Smith and Jennifer Watson
Illustrated by Jill Michelle Smith
Designed by Jennifer Watson

With special thanks to Dr David M.G. Waterhouse

Printed on 100% sustainably sourced, Carbon Balanced paper by Barnwell Print Ltd in association with World Land Trust. Helping to preserve critically threatened tropical rainforests.

WORLD
LAND
TRUST™
www.carbonbalancedprinter.com
Barnwell Print Reg. No. 2102
CHP019743

A catalogue record of this book is available from the British Library.